Forces

Contents

Revision

Did you know . . . ?

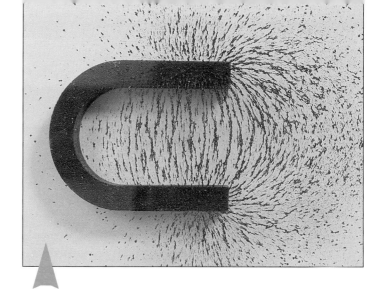

⭐ **Magnets can push or pull some things. Magnets can repel other magnets.**

⭐ **Gravity is a force which pulls things towards each other.**

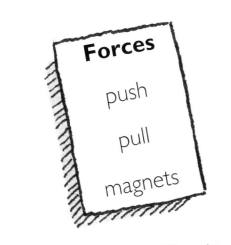

Task 1 Forces brainstorm

◆ **Think about . . .**

. . . the word **forces**.

✦ What do you know about forces?

✦ What other words do you think about when you think about forces?

✦ Brainstorm a list of words. Write them down.

◆ **When you have finished**

✦ Write each word on your list on separate pieces of paper.

✦ Keep the pieces of paper for Task 2 on page 3.

2

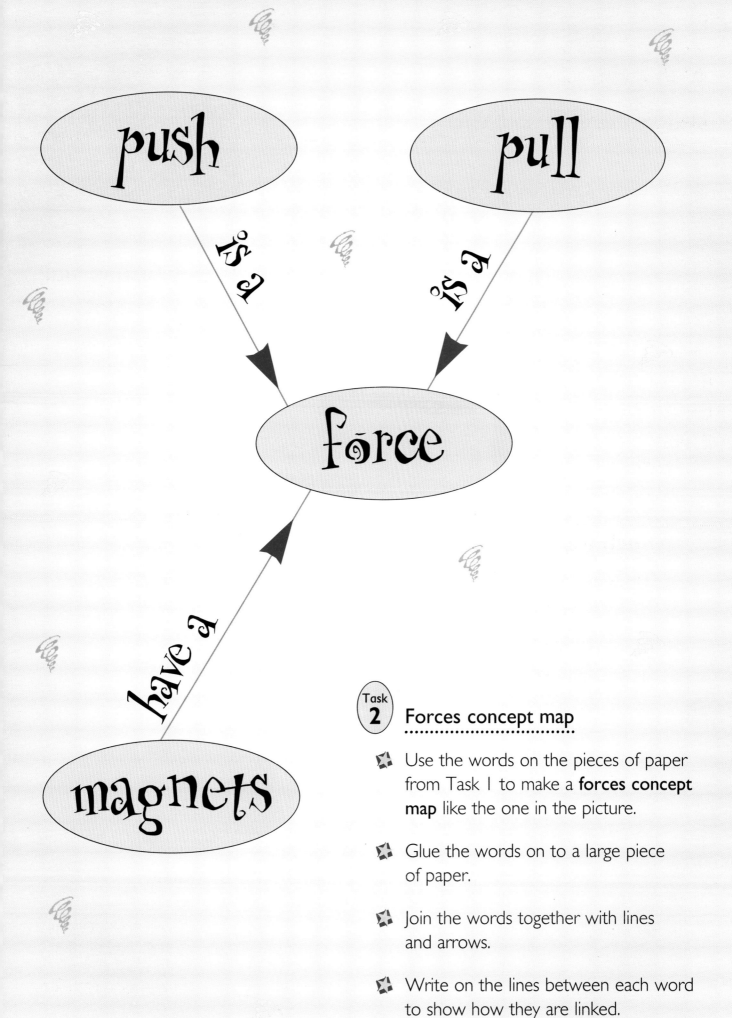

Task 2 — Forces concept map

- Use the words on the pieces of paper from Task 1 to make a **forces concept map** like the one in the picture.

- Glue the words on to a large piece of paper.

- Join the words together with lines and arrows.

- Write on the lines between each word to show how they are linked.

Where are the forces?

✪ Look at the photographs.

✪ What are the forces in action in each photograph?

✪ Write down your ideas.

✪ Make a table like this.

Photograph	Forces
Playing hockey	Man pushes hockey stick, hockey stick pushes ball

Forces and you

The bigger the push or pull force, the further something moves or the more the shape of something is changed.

A push or a pull force can change the shape of some things.

A push or a pull force can make something start to move.

Gravity is a force which pulls things towards Earth.

A pull force can stretch things.

A force is a push or a pull.

A force can make things slow down, go faster or stop.

Magnets can push or pull some things.

✪ Draw a strip cartoon of your day so far. Start with getting out of bed. Use Photocopy Master 1.

✪ Underneath each picture, write down the forces in action in the picture.

✪ Use the sentences from above.

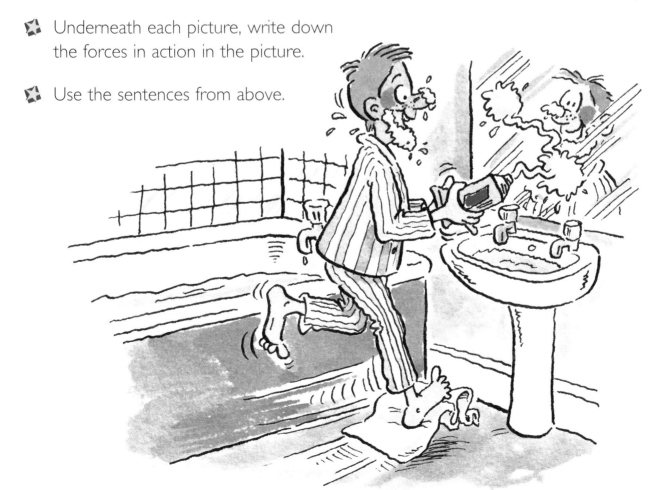

⭐ Forces can change the speed of things.

The robot is standing still. There are balanced forces.

The robot has been pushed over. This is an unbalanced force. He has moved and speeded up.

Task 5 Forces changing the speed of things

 PCM 2

 Draw some more pairs of pictures to show how a force can change the speed of something. Use Photocopy Master 2.

 Write a sentence underneath each picture to explain what is happening.

 Use these words:
forces
speed
balanced
unbalanced.

The basketball is still. There are balanced forces.

The player pushes the ball to the ground. The forces are unbalanced. The ball has speeded up.

The toy truck is still. There are balanced forces.

The child pulls the truck. The forces are unbalanced. The toy truck moves. It has speeded up.

What is speed?

A force is needed to make something move. When something begins to move, it goes somewhere. It travels a certain distance. It moves that distance over a certain amount of time.

That is **speed** – how far something moves in a certain amount of time.

Did you know . . ?

◀ **Speed** is how far something travels in a certain time.

Acceleration is when something begins to move, when something goes from being still to moving, or when something increases its speed or gets faster and faster.

We can measure speed.

- You might push a toy car and change its speed from 0 metres per second.

- It moves 10 metres in distance.

- It takes 10 seconds to move 10 metres. This is the time it takes.

- This can be shown as a sum:
  distance it travels ÷ time it takes = speed
  10 metres ÷ 10 seconds = 1.

This shows that the toy car goes 1 metre per second.

◆ Now try this

Working out speed

⋆ Work with a partner.

⋆ To help you, look back at the Fact File on page 7.

Challenge 1

Work out your speed if you walk for 10 seconds.
Don't forget to measure the distance.

Challenge 2

Work out your speed if you jog for 10 seconds.
Don't forget to measure the distance.

Challenge 3

Work out your speed if you run for 10 seconds.
Don't forget to measure the distance.

Challenge 4

Work out the speed of a toy wind-up car if it moves along the floor for 10 seconds.
Don't forget to measure the distance the toy car travels.

Fact File

Speed records

Did you know . . ?

The fastest flying bird is a peregrine falcon. It flies at 350 km an hour (217 miles an hour).

The fastest speed skater can reach speeds of over 44 km an hour (27 miles an hour).

The fastest greyhound can reach speeds of over 67 km an hour (41 miles an hour).

The fastest skier can reach speeds of over 241 km an hour (150 miles an hour).

The fastest racehorse can reach a speed of over 69 km an hour (43 miles an hour).

The fastest swimmer can reach speeds of over 8 km an hour (5 miles an hour).

Fact File

Measuring a pull force

Did you know . . ?

We can measure a pull force using a Newton meter. This is a type of force meter. You should have some Newton meters in your school. They are used to find out how much pull force it takes to make something move.

Look at the Newton meter in the photograph.

How do you think it works?

Task 7 — **Looking at Newton meters (force meters)**

 Get a Newton meter.

 Does it look like the one in the picture? How is it the same? How is it different?

 Try out the Newton meter. How much pull force does it take to make something move?

PCM 3

 Label the Newton meter on Photocopy Master 3. Make sure your labels explain what each part is for.

 Write a sentence to describe how a Newton meter works.

 Now try this

PCM 4

 Try the task on Photocopy Master 4.

Different kinds of Newton meters (force meters)

✵ Look at the photograph below.

✵ What is different about each of the Newton meters?

✵ Why do you think you need different kinds of Newton meters?

✵ What is the difference between the spring in the first Newton meter and the last Newton meter?

✵ What would you use the first Newton meter for?

✵ What would you use the last Newton meter for?

✵ Get some different Newton meters. Try them out around the classroom. Write down what happens.

PCM 5,6

✵ Which Newton meter will you use to move the different objects listed on Photocopy Master 5?

✵ Complete the table on Photocopy Master 6.

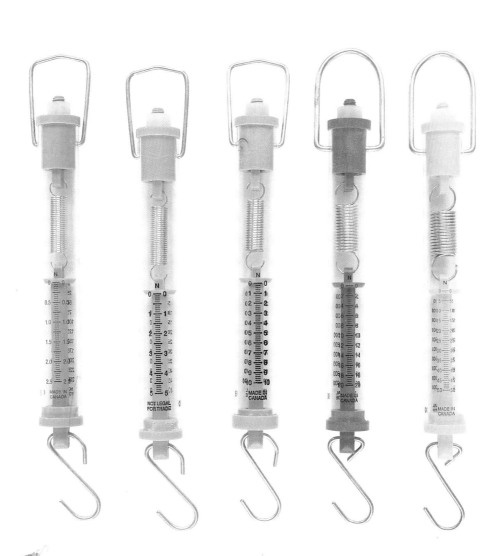

Friction is a force which slows things down.

Friction

Friction is a very important part of our everyday life.

So what is friction?
Friction happens when two surfaces move over each other. Friction slows things down.

> What is friction? I think it is a type of book.

Task 9 — Feeling friction

✪ Try this movement with your hands.

✪ Move the top hand sideways over the fingers of the hand underneath.
Keep the hand underneath still.

✪ What do you feel?
What happens to your fingers?
Why do you think this is?
Where are there push forces in action?

 PCM 7

✪ Look at the pictures on Photocopy Master 7.

✪ Write about what is happening.

Making friction

Get two hairbrushes or two combs.

Move one hairbrush or comb over the surface of the other hairbrush or comb.

What happens? Where are the push forces in action?

Write down your ideas.

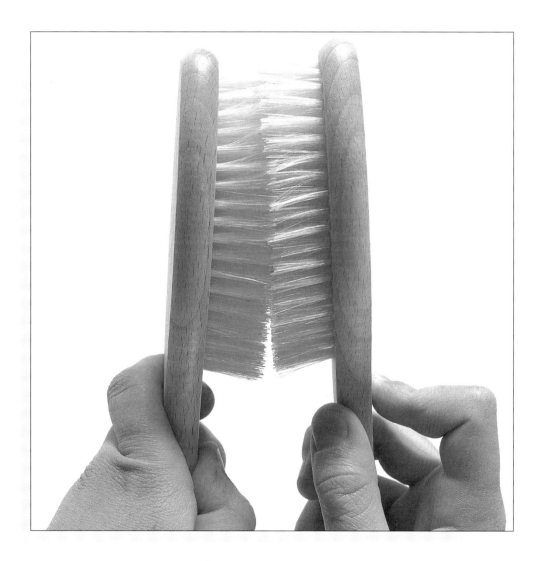

Did you notice how the bristles of the brushes are bending?

This is because they are pushing back against your push, making it harder to move them smoothly across each other.

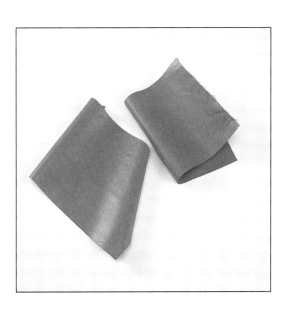

you need:

- two bricks
- two pieces of glass paper
- two pieces of silky fabric
- two pieces of rough fabric

Task II Feeling friction

⭐ Feel each of the objects.

⭐ Which will cause the most and least friction?

⭐ Why do you think this is?

⭐ Put the objects in order. Put the ones which make the most friction first and those which make the least friction last.

⭐ Move the objects over each other. Write down what you can feel and how the friction changes.

Friction around the classroom

⚜ Go around the classroom. Feel different surfaces. Decide how much friction you can feel against each surface.

⚜ Copy and complete the table.

Object	A lot of friction	A little friction	Almost no friction

◆ Now try this

⚜ Why do rainy days cause problems around the school?
Write down some ideas, using the information you know about friction.

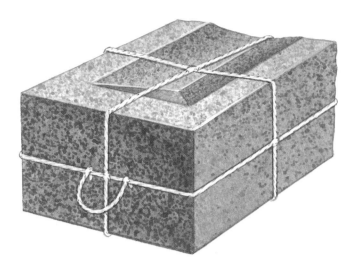

you need:

- a brick

- several Newton meters

- four different surfaces

- a team of Star Investigators

PLANNING BOARD

Our question _____

We will change _____

We will measure _____

We will keep _____
these things _____
the same to _____
make our test _____
fair _____

This is the
table we
will use.
(Put in the
headings.
Fill in the
left-hand
column.)

We will use _____
these things _____

Investigation

Measuring friction

☆ Design and plan an investigation to find out which surface has the most friction.

◆ Think about . . .

- How will you make sure the test is fair?

- How will you measure the friction force?

- Which Newton meter will you use?

- Will you need to repeat your measurements? Why?

- How will you record your results?

☆ Carry out the investigation.
Read the Newton meter carefully.

☆ Display your results. Will you use a bar chart or a line graph?

☆ Choose another surface that you have not tested.
Predict how big the friction force will be.
Try it out. Were you right?

☆ What do your results tell you?

Task **14** Investigation

Reducing friction

You need the same things as for Task 13, plus a tray.

Children in Class 6 were investigating this question.

Which is the best way to reduce friction?

Their challenge was to get the brick to the other side of the tray with the least amount of pull force.

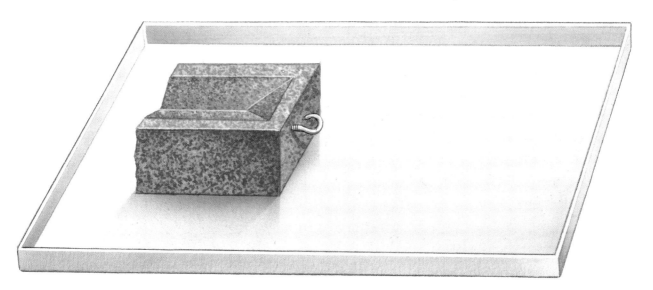

PLANNING BOARD

Our question _____

We will change _____

We will measure _____

We will keep _____
these things _____
the same to _____
make our test _____
fair _____

This is the
table we
will use.
(Put in the
headings.
Fill in the
left-hand
column.)

We will use _____
these things _____

✸ Plan and carry out an investigation to answer the question for Class 6.

✸ What could you use on the tray to reduce friction?

✸ When you have finished, write a set of instructions for Class 6, so that they can carry out your investigation.

 PCM 8

✸ Use Photocopy Master 8.

✸ At each stage, explain what forces are in action and how you are reducing friction.

(17)

trainers

court shoes

wellington boots

slippers

you need:

- some different shoes
- a Newton meter
- a team of Star Investigators

PLANNING BOARD

Our question _____
We will change _____
We will measure _____

We will keep _____
these things _____
the same to _____
make our test _____
fair _____

This is the table we will use. (Put in the headings. Fill in the left-hand column.)

We will use _____
these things _____

◆ Think about . . .

- Which Newton meter will you use?

- Will you need to repeat your measurements? How many times?

<table>
<tr><td>Task 15</td><td>

Investigation
Which shoe?

</td></tr>
</table>

- ✦ Collect four different shoes from your teacher.

- ✦ Which shoe would be best for wearing on an icy day?

- ✦ Write down the reason for your answer.

- ✦ Design and carry out an investigation to test this.

- ✦ Use a planning board to help you.

◆ When you have finished

- ✦ Draw a graph or chart using your results.

- ✦ Think about what kind of graph or chart it will be.

Use Photocopy Master 9 to show your graph or chart.

- ✦ Which shoe was the best?

- ✦ Why? Write down your answer.

- ✦ Talk about shoes. Why do we wear different shoes for different activities?

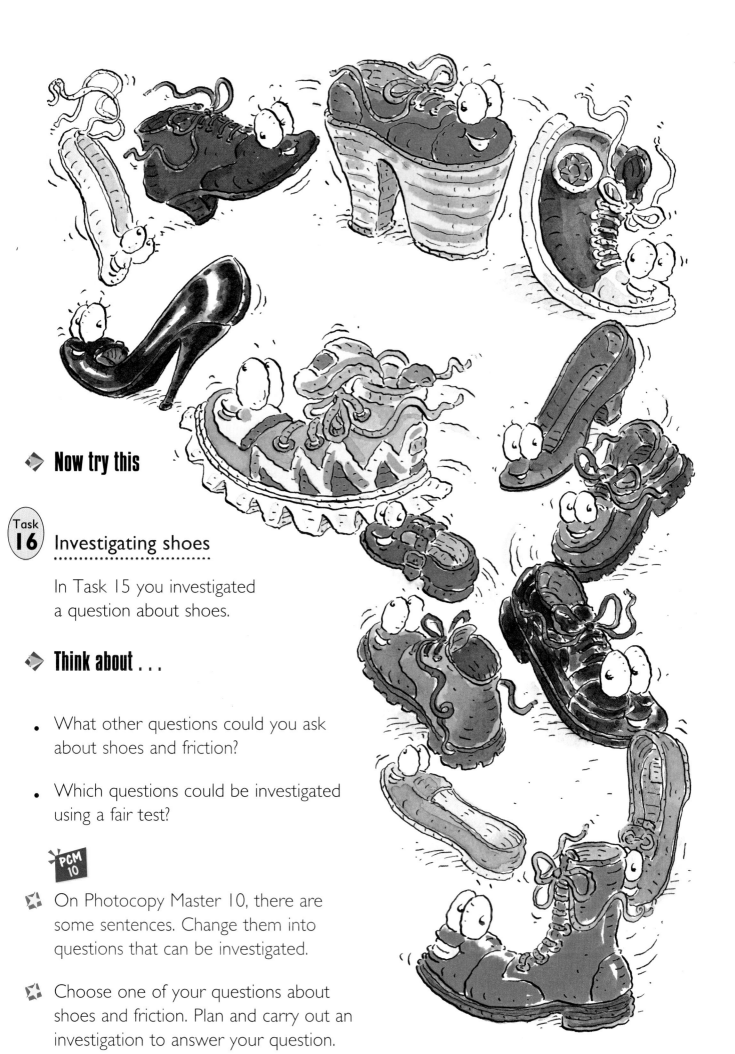

◆ Now try this

Task 16

Investigating shoes

In Task 15 you investigated
a question about shoes.

◆ Think about . . .

- What other questions could you ask
  about shoes and friction?

- Which questions could be investigated
  using a fair test?

PCM 10

- On Photocopy Master 10, there are
  some sentences. Change them into
  questions that can be investigated.

- Choose one of your questions about
  shoes and friction. Plan and carry out an
  investigation to answer your question.

1. handle bar grips

2. brakes

3. tyres

4. pedal

5. bike chain

 Task 17

Bikes and increasing friction

☼ Look at the photograph of the bike.

Each number is linked to a part of the bike.

☼ Write a sentence for each part of the bike, to explain how friction helps the rider of the bike.

☼ Fill in the table.

Place	Why and how friction is increased
handle bar grip	

Bikes and reducing friction

- Look at the photograph.

- What has the rider done to **reduce** friction so that he can race in the fastest time possible?

- Make a list of your ideas about reducing friction on a bike.

⭐ **If something does not move, then balanced forces are acting on it.**

Task 19 Tug of war

....

✪ Look at the cartoons.

✪ What kind of forces are in action?

✪ What would the children need to do to win the tug of war?

✪ Which picture shows an unbalanced force – where one child is pulling more than the other?

✪ Which pictures show where forces are balanced and no one is pulling more than the other?

✪ Draw pictures showing balanced and unbalanced forces on Photocopy Master 11.

Task 20 Bumbling clowns

 Imagine that you are a ringmaster at a circus.

✦ Use speech bubbles to explain to the audience the forces in action in the picture at the top.

✦ Draw your own picture to show what one clown has to do to push the other clown over.

✦ Use some speech bubbles to explain what is happening in your picture. Don't forget to talk about balanced and unbalanced forces.

● Look at the picture.

● Spot the balanced and unbalanced forces.

● How many different kinds of forces can you find?

● Write down your answers on a table.

What is happening in the picture?	Balanced force or unbalanced force?

Task 22 Balanced and unbalanced forces – floating and sinking

you need:

- a plastic tank filled with water

- an inflated balloon

✦ Try this. Carefully push an inflated balloon into the water.

✦ What do you feel?

✦ What does it feel like the water is doing to the balloon?

✦ Write a sentence about what happens and what it feels like.

✦ You are using a push force to force the balloon into the water. What do you feel the water is doing to the balloon?

The water is pushing the balloon back up.
We can use arrows to show the direction of the force and how big the force is.

✦ Now let go of the balloon. What happens? Why?

you need:

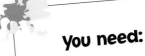

- a plastic tank filled with water
- a stone
- an elastic band
- a Newton meter

⚠ **Safety point:** Do not drop the stone in the tank. It could break or damage the tank.

Testing a stone in water (with an elastic band)

✸ Hold the stone in the air.

✸ Look at the elastic band.

✸ Now put the stone into the water.

✸ Watch the elastic band. What happens to it?

✸ Draw a picture to show what you think happens to the stone and the elastic band when you put the stone in the water. Use arrows to help you explain.

✸ What would **you** have to do to make the elastic the same length as it is in the water? What does this tell you about what the water is doing?

Task **24**

Testing a stone in water (with a Newton meter)

✸ Now weigh the stone using a Newton meter. Write down the weight (the pull down towards Earth).

✸ Keep the stone hooked to the Newton meter and lower the stone into the water.

✸ The reading on the Newton meter changes. Why do you think this is?

✸ Draw and write to show what you think happens to the stone when it is put in the water. Use arrows to help you explain.

The push force of water

Did you know . . ?

Water has a push force. It is called 'up-thrust'.

If something floats on water, the push down force is the same as the up-thrust (push up force) of the water.

The forces are balanced when something floats, so the two arrows are the same.

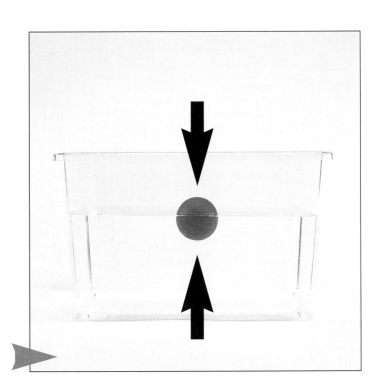

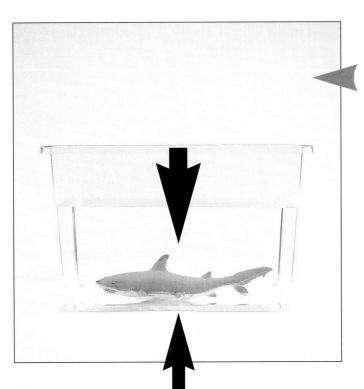

As something sinks, the push force (weight) of the object is greater than the water.

The up-thrust of the water is less than the push down (weight) of the object, so the object sinks.

The forces are unbalanced as it is sinking, so one arrow is bigger than the other.

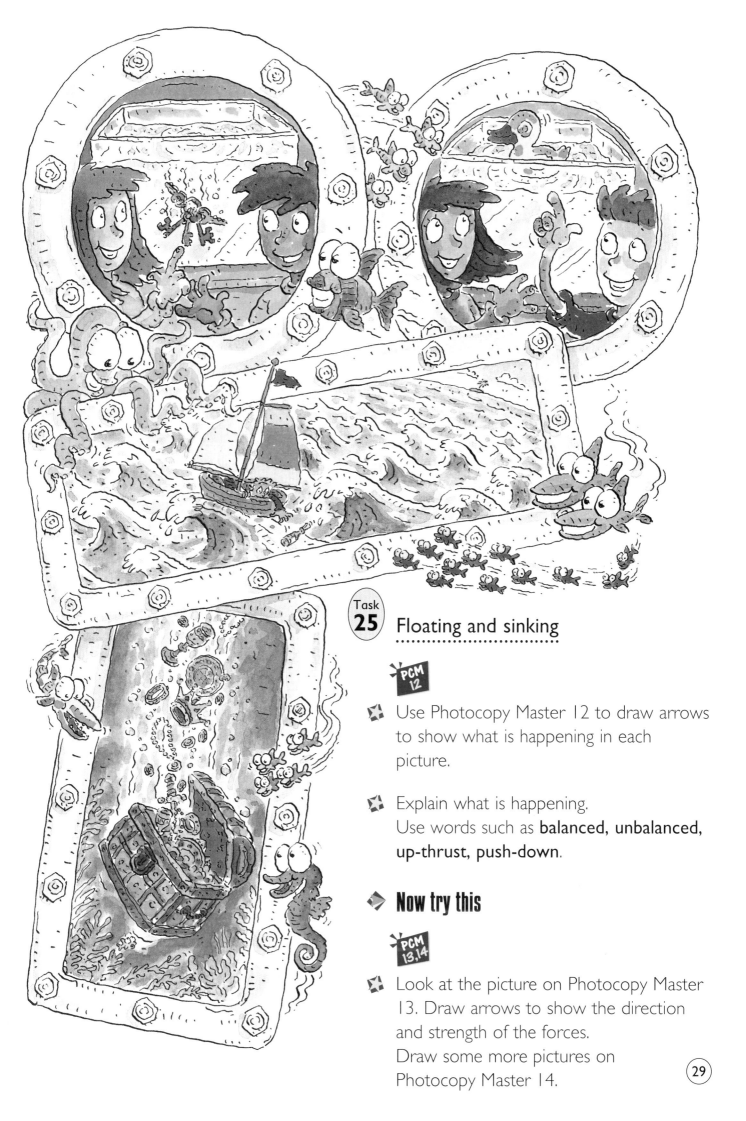

Task 25 Floating and sinking

PCM 12

★ Use Photocopy Master 12 to draw arrows to show what is happening in each picture.

★ Explain what is happening.
Use words such as **balanced, unbalanced, up-thrust, push-down**.

◆ Now try this

PCM 13,14

★ Look at the picture on Photocopy Master 13. Draw arrows to show the direction and strength of the forces.
Draw some more pictures on Photocopy Master 14.

Fact File

Putting friction to work

Roads on hills can be dangerous as cars and lorries sometimes travel down them too fast.
On some very steep hills there are **escape lanes**.
These are special lanes at the side of the road which are made from material which slows the car or lorry down, so that they can stop safely.

**The Highway Committee
County Hall
DURHAM**

Class 6
Clairview School
Clairview Road
DURHAM

25 May 1997

Dear Class 6

The Highway Committee has decided to create an 'escape lane' on the A146, which has a very steep hill, six miles from Durham. As you know, escape lanes are made with special materials which slow lorries and cars down.

The Committee would like you to investigate which materials to use for this escape lane.

You must provide evidence to support your conclusions.

We look forward to receiving your results.

Yours sincerely

A.Carter (Dr)
Chair, Highways Committee

 Task 26

Planning an escape lane

✦ Plan and carry out an investigation to answer the question from the Highways Committee.

✦ Use a planning board to help you.

◆ Think about . . .

• Which materials will you test?

• What will you measure?

• Will you need to repeat your measurements?

• How will you make it a fair test?

• What type of table will you draw?

✦ Carry out the investigation.

✦ Measure carefully and record your results.

◆ When you have finished

✦ Write a report for the Highways Committee.

◆ Think about . . .

• What information will they need?

• Do you need to draw a graph so that they can see the results more easily?

• How will you explain your results to the Committee?

◆ Now try this

PCM 15

✦ Try the task on Photocopy Master 15.

Checkpoint

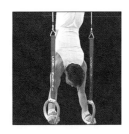

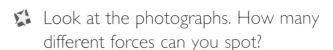

Task 27 Spotting the forces

✦ Look at the photographs. How many different forces can you spot?

- A force is a push or a pull.

- A push or a pull force can make something start to move.

- A push or a pull can change the shape of something.

- The bigger the push or pull force, the further something moves or the more the shape of something is changed.

- A pull force can stretch things.

- A force can make things slow down, go faster or stop.

- Gravity is a force which pulls things towards each other.

- Forces can change the speed of things.

- Friction is a force which slows things down.

- If something does not move, balanced forces are acting upon it.

PCM 16

✦ Use Photocopy Master 16 to show your ideas.